TESTS:
Marked For Life?

S. Alan Cohen

Scholastic

Scholastic Canada Ltd.
123 Newkirk Road, Richmond Hill, Ontario, Canada L4C 3G5

Scholastic Inc.
730 Broadway, New York, NY 10003, USA

Ashton Scholastic Limited
Private Bag 1, Penrose, Auckland 6, New Zealand

Ashton Scholastic Pty Limited
PO Box 579, Gosford, NSW, 2250, Australia

Scholastic Publications Ltd.
Holly Walk, Leamington Spa, Warwickshire CV32 4LS, England

Cover photo © Masterfile/Daily Telegraph

Canadian Cataloguing in Publication Data

Cohen, S. Alan
    Tests: Marked for life?

(Bright Idea)
Bibliography: p.
ISBN 0-590-71857-6

1. Educational tests and measurement - Evaluation.
2. Psychological tests - Evaluation. 3. Grading and
marking. (Students) - Evaluation. I. Title. II. Series.

LB3060.8.C63 1988   371.2'6013   C87-094903-9

76543   Printed in Hong Kong   1 2 3 4 5/9

To millions of kids whose parents didn't know better.
To educators who should know better and don't.
To Shelley, whose parents knew better.
To Laney, Michael, Amelia and others on the way whose
*   grandparents know better.*
To Adrian who knows a good idea when he sees one.
And to Joan.

Contents

Preface

Please do me a favor. Push the imaginary *Reset* button that will clear memory in your brain. Not everything, of course. Just the ideas and feelings you may have stored away about any of the following:

test — criterion test — norm referenced standardized test — grade levels — dumb — smart — IQ — aptitude — learn — teach

Thanks. Now we can begin to take a fresh look at some old ideas.

Alan Cohen
Spring, 1987
San Francisco

The psyche you save may be your own

People are dangerous

This book is about tests. Most tests are innocent pieces of printed paper. The trouble is, they're often misused by well-meaning educators. Such misuse has hurt my children, will probably hurt my grandchildren, and continues to hurt my students. Educators don't mean to hurt us. And they wouldn't hurt us if they and the public knew just a little bit more about what school tests do, and what they can't do.

We've been obsessed with school tests since around World War I. This obsession, combined with a ubiquitous ignorance *about* school tests, has hurt millions of students. Perhaps if we could understand just a bit more, the next generation of students might be saved from the astounding waste of talent, worry and money that misusers of tests have caused over the last 60 years. If we act fast enough, perhaps part of this generation can be spared.

Two types of tests

Schools use tests for three reasons:

- They want to compare us with others.
- They want to see what we know or can do.
- They want to do both.

We call the first kind of test *norm referenced* because the test score is compared with or referenced to some *norm*. The norm is used to tell how well we do compared with others. Hence the name *Norm Referenced Standardized Test* — NRST for short.

My own teachers called the second type just plain *test*. If it was ominously important, they majestically announced it as an *exam*. A routine Friday ritual was merely a *quiz*. A surprise quiz was a *pop quiz*. Mr.

Donovan, my eleventh grade history teacher (in those days it was history, not social studies), called them *Can Do Tests*. The teacher who presided over the terrifying French sessions next door to Mr. Donovan called hers *Can't Do Tests*. (She didn't get along with Mr. Donovan.)

But that is a bygone era — ancient educational history. Today the "in" term is CRT, which stands for *Criterion Referenced Test*. Some people call these Can Do Tests instructional or curriculum referenced tests.

To summarize the difference between the two: CRTs are (supposed to be) "referenced" to what was actually taught; NRSTs are referenced to other victims' scores. The names tell the stories.

You can't tell the difference by test items

Here is a Can Do Test item. It tests how well you can do after being taught that 2 x 3 = 6.

TEST ITEM: 2 x 3 = ?

Now for the difference. Here is an item from an NRST designed to see how you compare with others in doing multiplication.

TEST ITEM: 2 x 3 = ?

Do you get the point? No difference. The same item can be used to tell what we learned and how well we learned compared with others. The real difference between NRST and CRT items lies in what teachers or psychologists make of them and do with them. That's when all the trouble starts, when people make decisions about other people's lives based on these tests.

Look out for two dangers

Danger 1: The test score may be *unreliable*. For example, on Monday you might score as well as 50% of your peers on an NRST of your sexual sensitivity. But on Tuesday, if we retested you, you might be a raging rabbit in heat, scoring higher than 99% of your peers. And if we'd tested you two days before Monday, you might have scored as well as an eleven-day-old corpse, somewhere below 99% of your peers.

This is an unreliable test, because we can't trust the score. The tendency is to blame the lousy test — or your sexual sensitivity for not standing still. And that would make sense if test reliability were a problem to estimate. The fact is that test reliability is easy to estimate. So the blame lies with the people who make decisions on the basis of unreliable test scores. Either they don't bother to check the reliability, or they ignore the unreliability. In either case, they mislabel you dead, average or a "manifest raging libido-type," depending on which day you took the test, or what time of the day you took the test, or what you did just before taking the test, or any of an infinite number of events that cause test scores to vary.

Danger 2: Even though test experts consider a test reliable (that is, accurate), it may be *invalid*. Test validity refers to the degree to which the test measures what the test user thinks it measures. You wouldn't want a school to make decisions about your child based on a test that doesn't really measure what it sets out to measure, would you? But schools do! How often? Usually!

Here's what muddies the water:

- Most tests *look* as if they measure what they claim to measure.
- Test experts have a forgiving definition of accuracy.

Testers have a method of establishing reliability for highly inaccurate tests. So they end up with a reliable but not very accurate score of *something* — often not what they think it is! If all that twists your mind, it's meant to.

Untwisting the twister

Assume you take our "Test of Sexual Sensitivity," a 50-item true or false questionnaire that asks the kind of titillating questions often found in *Playboy* or *Playgirl* magazines, or, in less explicit form, in your local newspaper's Sunday magazine section. Assume also that test experts have established its reliability. Reliability means that, on the average, a *group's* average test score stays about the same when we administer the test again and again at different times of the day, on different days, and under reasonably variant conditions. Note, however, that the scores of *individual* members of the group will vary considerably.

Now assume your shrink decides that, based on this test, you should take a sex drive depressant pill because your score was greater than 99% of others in your age group, and that means your libido has run amuck.

Obviously the problem is not the questionnaire; it's the bird brain who jumps from a pencil-paper questionnaire response to conclusions about how you would behave toward attractive or (considering your supposedly unrestrained libido) unattractive members of the opposite sex. In this example, the danger is to assume (1) that people's verbal descriptions of their own behaviors are accurate, and (2) that just because the group's average score is reliable, your individual score is accurate. These assumptions are probably untrue. The printed test is not dangerous. People, not paper, make trouble.

When test scores are unstable, they are considered *unreliable*. When professionals make dumb decisions based on unreliable (or even reliable) test results, we say the test is *invalid*. What we really mean is the *decisions* are invalid.

And so...

...test invalidity and unreliability are the dangers discussed in the following chapters. When you finish reading them, you'll know more about tests than many professionals who use them do, and that could give you an advantage when dealing with the widespread misuse of tests.

This knowledge is important, because the psyche you save may be your own, or your kid's.

Guaranteed failure: the great absurdity

From reading chapter one, you will remember that:

- NRSTs and CRTs are two kinds of tests.
- NRSTs compare us with others.
- CRTs tell what we learned.
- Usually we can't tell CRT items from NRST items.
- *Reliability* refers to how stable a test score is.
- *Validity* refers to what the test really measures.
- *Reliability* is easy to estimate.
- *Validity* depends on what humans do with test scores.
- Test makers are more or less innocent technicians, but test users can be dangerous.

If you learned these nine things, you'll get a perfect score on this CRT:

A Can Do Test

1. What are the two types of tests described in the chapter?
2. Which type reports your score in terms of its comparison with others?
3. Your teacher expects you to have learned how to appreciate literature. To test that, which type of test would be used, an NRST or a CRT?
4. Here is a test item: "Name the capital of Iowa." Is this an NRST or a CRT item?
5. If you are not sure this Can Do Test really tests what you learned in the chapter, you are questioning the test's (choose one)
   a. reliability.
   b. validity.
6. If you are not sure the score you earn on this test is your true score, you are questioning the test's (choose one)
   a. reliability.
   b. validity.
7. Which is easier to estimate, reliability or validity?
8. Validity is a quality of (choose the best one)
   a. a printed test.
   b. a human's interpretation of test results.
   c. test length.
   d. test difficulty.
9. Which are more dangerous, tests or test users?

The purpose makes a difference

Notice how "easy" that Can Do Test was. You probably got all the items correct.

Call it telepathy or whatever you wish, but I can hear your thoughts resounding across the continent: "But you gave us the answers. You made it easy!" Spoken like a true product of the Euro-American school, which is less concerned with learning and more concerned with discriminating haves from have nots.

The purpose of this book is to teach you about tests. Its purpose is not to make the learning easy or difficult; its purpose is to make learning *happen*. So we started this chapter by finding out if it had happened. It doesn't matter how easy the test was. What matters is that you understood chapter one, which we think is necessary for understanding chapter two.

When we teach, it's important to make sure students master what we intend them to learn. Lots of kids in school are lost in chapter one while the teacher is already covering chapter two. Some are left permanently behind the eight ball.

Don't confuse CRTs and NRSTs

One major purpose of a CRT is to see what learning has occurred — or, from the opposite point of view, to find out what hasn't been learned so we can teach it. How is that different from an NRST? That's one of the most important points in this book.

CRTs often *appear* to be easier because we design our instruction to match the test. The teacher (we suppose) wants everyone to learn. So the teacher rigs it for everyone to learn by making sure that what is tested is taught, or what is taught is tested.

NRSTs appear to be harder because their primary purpose is to differentiate among test takers. We want NRSTs to rank kids (or adults) from best to least best. We *want* some kids to fail! If everyone gets all the NRST items correct, the test can't differentiate and we have no rank. Everyone is first, and apparently that's not what most people want!

To state it bluntly, NRSTs are designed to divide us into haves and have nots — and many points between. The more points it can divide us into, the better the NRST. We say the test is "very sensitive."

The purpose of teaching, on the other hand, is for *everyone* to learn what is taught, and the CRT's purpose is to check for learning. If teaching is effective and the CRT does its job, the fewer points it divides us into, the better the CRT.

The great absurdity

Confusing NRSTs and CRTs contributes to the great school absurdity. If the purpose of NRSTs is to differentiate and rank, then using NRSTs to make teaching decisions redefines teaching as a method of ranking and differentiating. It compels teaching decisions that will make sure some students haven't learned! Absurd!

But that absurdity has taken hold, unfortunately. The growing obsession with NRSTs over the last 60 years has a lot of people convinced that only a few students will ever be excellent, an equal number will fail, and the largest number will be mediocre. In fact, many schools have formal policies that forbid everyone from learning everything! They don't want equality; they want haves, mild haves, and have nots. Perhaps it's the North American way. It certainly has been the way for the French, the Dutch and the British.

Consider: I write a book (design a course) to teach you about tests. I don't intend or expect all of you to learn. I consciously write (and teach) so some of you will not learn at all, most of you will learn some but not all, and the book (my course) will succeed smashingly with a few of you. I teach and test for differences. Isn't that absurd?

If this is the model then we have to have a failure rate that makes the cover of Newsweek

Can you imagine physicians practicing medicine or lawyers practicing law using the same model? Certainly physicians expect some patients to die; lawyers expect to lose some cases; teachers expect to fail with some students (although we usually fail the recalcitrant student, not the teacher). But it's quite another story for a physician to practice medicine in a way that ensures some patients *must* die, most must feel "just okay," and very few will feel healthy. How shocking to expect lawyers to premeditatively practice so two-thirds of their clients *must* win small settlements, 16% must lose their cases, and 16% will win materially.

Yet the educational community has agreed to practice its profession in just that way — about 16% will learn everything expected, 68% will learn just enough to survive school, and 16% will fail. This absurdity is not inevitable. It's policy!

Contrast this policy with a CRT approach. I prepared to teach you nine things in chapter one. Notice the CRT had nine items. Notice the review preceding the CRT had nine items. Notice how effective chapter one was in teaching those nine things. (Please allow me that breach of humility.) I expect every reader to have learned it all. There's no discrimination because everyone gets an A.

Now consider what NRSTs have wrought. If we believe in NRSTs, which are designed to demonstrate inequalities, then sooner or later schooling will be shaped to conform to NRST expectations. We should not be surprised, then, if most graduates of our schools are mediocre, and significant numbers are illiterate. As my old coach used to say: "We gets what we wants."

Striving for unequal results is so deeply entrenched in western schools that we truly believe everyone can *not* learn everything we teach in school. In fact, we guarantee that result. We rig it: few...most...few.

Are CRTs really easier than NRSTs?

Of course not. CRTs only look that way when teachers use them to ensure that all the kids learn. If I design a test of what I expect you to learn, and thoroughly teach what I test, and expect you to learn it, then when the test items appear there'll be no surprises. They'll test precisely what I teach. Thus, for those who are taught, CRTs look easy. For those not taught, they look just as tough as most NRSTs.

But contrast CRTs with NRSTs. If the NRST's purpose is to rank test takers from low to high, then either we must teach ineffectively, or we must sneak into the test something that will ensure a ranking even when we teach effectively. In other words, we must include among the test items things that weren't taught, things that only some test takers have had a chance to learn on their own. Then we'll get a ranking, even when we teach effectively.

So, the difference between NRSTs and CRTs...

...boils down to this simple fact: NRSTs must have items, or factors hidden in items, that have not been effectively taught. In contrast, CRTs must be referenced to what has been effectively taught. The NRST *must* make students different. If they've been taught well, the CRT makes them more alike.

From selection to natural selection

A peek at the history of NRSTs explains the great absurdity — although, alas, it doesn't lessen it.

Early in this century a French physician, Binet, developed a test to sort those children who would be allowed into secondary schools from those who would be shunted to more mundane destinies. The purpose of the test was to discriminate, not to assess teaching nor to monitor learning. An American version of that test eventually became the famous Stanford Binet Intelligence Test.

At the advent of World War I, the American government also developed a selection device, a tool designed to discriminate among the millions of young men entering military service. It selected the lucky ones from the cannon fodder. Again the purpose was to discriminate, not to monitor either instruction or learning. That test became the *Otis Quick Scoring Test of Mental Abilities*, used in public schools for decades. The Otis yielded a score called the "intelligence quotient."

How school and military selection tests became known as intelligence tests is a mystery, but I have a theory.

Perhaps the academicians who developed those measures didn't realize their products were made in their own images, so to speak. In other words, university types can be expected to develop scholastic discriminators — tests on which they themselves will perform well. But how did they get other people to accept their criteria as the social standards? How was their way legitimized as *the* way? "Divine right" was discredited by the French, American and scientific revolutions. But there was Plato with his myth of the philosopher king, of the "innate quality of superior intellect." Perfect for legitimizing the use of such instruments as discriminators of human beings.

Calling "it" the skills and knowledge needed to succeed in school would not have been as ego boosting or awe inspiring as calling it intelligence, which sounds like a naturally and genetically endowed gift.

I can't prove my theory, but I do know that those selection devices have nurtured a belief that has a tenacious hold on the western psyche. No one seems to question that some of us are born with more of that "thing" than others, and that we need tests to identify it. Tests have resulted in all sorts of inclusions and exclusions. Today, western democracies generate a double elite: those born rich, and those born with what most people believe are genetically endowed superior powers. Often people confuse the two; they assume that those born rich also have that natural endowment, or that those assumed to have that endowment are either born rich or destined to become rich. In a society that pays lip service to science and democracy, natural endowment is a convenient substitute for divine right.

NRSTs that discriminate

I offer you a wide selection: college board SATs; all intelligence tests; tests used for entry into private schools, universities and professional schools; aptitude tests; tests of creative abilities; tests of cognitive development; graduate record exams; national nursing exams; national teachers exams; tests to discriminate the gifted; Miller's Analogies Test — the list is endless. Scores of commercially and locally developed NRSTs feed the natural endowment myth.

In America, Jefferson has triumphed. He believed that a public school system would train a new aristocracy; its modern driving force is the NRST. In Canada and western European democracies, just as in totalitarian societies, the NRST preserves an aristocracy that no revolution has ever eliminated.

An opposing view of education

By the end of this book, perhaps you'll consider another view of testing and schooling, one driven by the idea of a universal natural endowment. Two truths stand out:

- Although they vary in their learning rates, all human beings have an unlimited capacity to learn.
- Their ability to teach others is also unlimited.

These truths call for a different view of testing. In this book, that view is represented by the CRT.

Review

- NRSTs are designed primarily to select the best learners, the worst learners, and all learners in between. They do it by including items that are untaught, or likely have been taught ineffectively.

- CRTs are designed primarily to measure learning, or to measure what needs to be learned, or to measure the effects of teaching. They are supposed to measure precisely what is taught, and when preceded by sound instruction, yield fewer differences in results.

- The "great school absurdity" is the idea that teachers' efforts should result in a large degree of mediocrity and smaller degrees of failure and success. This deliberate policy has most people believe that intelligence is genetically determined. The policy has been promoted by self-serving college professors who tend to do well on their own tests.

Having learned these points, everyone gets an A for chapter two. Now on to chapter three, where we'll see what happens when we try to make NRSTs act like CRTs.

Who needs a lousy football game!

What's wrong with tests? Nothing that some test knowledge wouldn't cure. Tests aren't the problem; people are. People often misuse tests. The problems come from decisions people make based on test scores.

To be sure, some tests are bad because they are made by amateurs. But they're harmless if the test users understand what the tests tell them. Even tests created by experts are inherently harmless. What we do with them makes them dangerous.

An educational test is like a monkey wrench. In one person's hand it stops a leak, in another's it causes a leak, in a third it fractures a skull. We can't blame a test for hurting us any more than we can blame a monkey wrench.

How are educational tests misused?

They usually don't test what we think they test, and test users misinterpret their results: a *validity* problem. Or the scores are inaccurate, but test users act as if they're not: a *reliability* problem.

Combining CRTs and NRSTs

You will recall that we can divide tests into two types: NRSTs and CRTs. We *could* also combine the two, but so far no one has done it well.

Most schools use commercially published NRSTs. Commercial publishers pretend their NRSTs are both CRTs and NRSTs. They don't come right out and say so, but they allow their customers to think so, because it's what the customers want. Over the last decade some teachers and administrators have begun to suspect that testing should have something to do with instructional decision making, that tests measuring *exactly* what schools teach might prove useful for monitoring quality control. But commercially published tests are NRSTs, not combinations of the two.

Unfortunately, schools aren't always sure what they teach. In fact, a book titled *A Place Called School* and several recent issues of *Phi Delta Kappan* have argued that most schools are very fuzzy about what kids learn in their classrooms. "Critical thinking," "reading comprehension," "phonics," "understanding the causes of the Cold War" may well be worthwhile learning outcomes, but no one is quite sure exactly what those impressive outcomes look like. "No one," unfortunately, includes teachers and students.

Are we talking cultural literacy?

Fuzzies, and the great mismatch

A wise man once told me: "You can't test a fuzzy." For example, what did my teacher mean when he claimed to have taught us "to understand and appreciate the great Melville novel, *Moby Dick*"? He admonished us to remember what the bearded Ahab must have looked like as he hobbled about the poop deck with lightning flashing above him. But on the test he asked: "How would you feel if you confronted the whale that had destroyed your leg?"

What he admonished and what he tested were both related to the fuzzy outcome — "understanding and appreciating" Melville's work. However, the question didn't test what he taught. It's as if he asked us to plant an apple orchard and then count the number of oranges on the trees to judge the success of our planting. The discouraging fact is that most people accept this kind of mismatch as the norm; that is, they expect to be taught one thing and measured on another.

It's easy to recognize that a mismatch between what is taught and what is tested is the norm rather than the exception. However, do you also recognize how it ensures that only a few will be excellent, an equal number will fail, and the rest of us will waddle about in mediocrity when test time comes? Had we been thoroughly prepared to express how we would feel if we were confronting the whale that had chewed off our leg, all of us would have scored perfectly on that test item.

By providing fuzzy definitions of instructional outcomes, we increase the probability of mismatch. Mismatch, in turn, ensures *chance* results on tests. When teaching doesn't guarantee that everyone will answer correctly, we get a chance (normal) distribution of test scores.

Consider another example. "Understanding the causes of the Cold War" appears to be a reasonable outcome of a social studies unit. Pretend I wanted to teach to that understanding and use a CRT item to monitor the effect of my efforts. Were I to teach thoroughly for a written test, I would make sure that every student had written a 150-word composition that met my criteria. The test would then ask students to write a similar 150-word composition to demonstrate that they understood the causes of the Cold War. In other words, I would teach precisely what I wanted to test.

However, if I wanted to ensure a normal distribution of scores on that same test, there'd be no writing or critiquing beforehand. Instead, I would talk about it, perhaps even demonstrate how to do it. But I certainly wouldn't have each student write a paper to my satisfaction before giving the test. To do so would guarantee perfect scores. To avoid perfect scores I have to avoid perfect teaching so that some will do poorly, most reasonably well, and a few superbly.

There's a real gut issue here. Leaving aside, for the moment, the question of how to agree on what is worth teaching, let's go back to the idea that effective instruction ensures that what is taught is precisely what is tested. Apparently schools perceive their mission to be discriminating among students more than providing effective instruction, and that perception has become so fundamental to the school culture that testing what we teach and teaching what we test is viewed by many educators as cheating!

Fuzzy outcomes and the resulting mismatches between what is taught and what is tested allow us to maintain the myth of innate scholastic ability. After all, since we didn't teach it, it must have come from the genes.

No one has more of a stake in maintaining this system than commercial test makers. Consider the infinite variations of teaching activities that could be subsumed under the two fuzzies "understanding and appreciating Melville's novel" and "understanding the causes of the Cold War." Now consider the impossibility of a commercial test maker testing either outcome with test items that match every teacher's unique and precise definition of those outcomes. Test makers prefer the less-than-perfect teaching that characterizes most classrooms. As long as we hold to the myth that fuzzy outcomes are more important than specific outcomes, commercial NRSTs can make money.

Trying to make a buck

Making money in the school test market today requires a sales pitch that claims NRSTs have CRT characteristics, which is a legally safe way to give customers the impression that they are current with the times. Notice, test publishers don't claim their NRSTs *are* CRTs, just that they have some of the features. The times are beginning to demand CRTs.

What are some of these features? According to such companies, their test makers review the current textbooks and curriculum guides to find what is being taught. Then, goes the claim, they make test items to fit what they find. This washes with educators because most of them don't know very much about the science of testing — and because they're already so used to planting apple trees and counting oranges. The mismatch is the norm.

So test publishers are secure in the knowledge that those who buy and use their NRSTs don't appreciate that even very small differences among what different classrooms teach as phonics, or multiplication, or literature appreciation, or anything else, invalidates those NRSTs as criterion tests of learning.

I suppose that in capitalist societies commercial NRST publishers have a right to make a buck as long as they don't break the law or lie. But the public also has a duty to demand that their professional educators not be so gullible.

What, then, do NRSTs test?

Standardized reading or math achievement NRSTs certainly are not testing precisely what teachers teach. Nor are they testing innate ability or any naturally endowed power. They are testing some general "how to succeed in school and life" behaviors, as well as smatterings of learned skills that are part of a body of behaviors called reading, or math, or phonics, or science, or whatever a test claims to measure. Standardized achievement tests sample from among that body's specific behaviors, and we call the resulting measure an achievement test. We will discuss the "how to succeed in school and life" behaviors in a later chapter. For now, let's consider what gets lost when NRSTs sample those vast bodies of behaviors tested in such achievement tests.

Precision gets lost. NRSTs are compromises. When we try to make one test for the nation that will measure the myriad of things thousands of teachers are teaching, we can't be specific. If we knew exactly what was taught, we would construct a CRT to measure what was learned, looking for a near-perfect match between the two. The compromise is to "sample" from the body of multiple behaviors we think relate to an area of achievement, such as reading or math.

A general, insensitive, sluggish measure

The result is a general measure of what schools, or teachers, are doing — useful, because it allows us to compare the performance of a class, or a school, or any group, with a national or regional norm. We can tell if, in general, the average score of a group of tested students is

Prof Educators Don't mandate the tests, Politicians do

above, below or equal to the norm. But note the
important word: *group*.

However useful it may be in describing a group, an
NRST doesn't provide a reliable picture of an individual
score, especially if the student is above or below the
average. And more importantly, it's an *insensitive* and
sluggish measure of instructional outcome, whether we're
measuring an individual or a group.

What does *insensitive* mean? If teachers try to use the
reports of commercially published NRSTs to make
decisions about what to teach, or if curriculum experts try
to use NRST results to guide their decisions about
modifying curriculum, they find little help. Simply
knowing that a group, a class, a school, or a school
system is below national norms in a general area such as
reading is not much of a guide for teachers and
curriculum supervisors.

Test scores don't tell what must be taught. Nor do
they tell how or when. They merely tell what all but the
most comatose teacher already knows — in general, the
group is very good, or average, or hopeless.

An NRST is *sluggish* because whatever redundant
information it can deliver lags too far behind the action,
the daily activities of teaching and learning. Such a test is
usually given once a year. The results are delivered at
least weeks, and usually months, later. In many schools
the teachers rarely see the results.

Even if they did, they couldn't use them to plan
instruction because:

- individual scores aren't reliable;
- the group score is already known, if not by number,
  at least by the general category of high, low or
  average;
- the results don't indicate precisely what must be
  learned.

Classroom action shifts daily. NRST data come

No possible teacher response to scores

annually. That's sluggish monitoring. Imagine monitoring the heart of a cardiac patient with a system that reports once a year. Imagine running a business with a bookkeeping system that monitors only once a year. Ridiculous!

So what good are standardized achievement tests?

Some of us have been asking that for years. Nevertheless, most American school systems purchase them, to the tune of over a million dollars annually. The major use is exactly that described in the previous chapter: people use NRSTs to include students in, or exclude them from, certain educational opportunities. They do this even though the individual test scores are unreliable, and they know it. Meanwhile, commercial NRST publishers and many educators pretend NRSTs are also CRTs — and we all know that isn't so.

Back to CRTs

How wonderful if schools used tests of exactly what was taught, administered as a daily, integral part of instruction. Then everyone would know precisely what was learned, who learned it when, what methods or materials worked or didn't work. How wonderful to dream of such tests driving the instructional program on a daily basis — no sluggish delay between teaching and testing. And how wonderful it would be if, in addition to instructionally referenced tests, we had norms to tell what percentage of students at different ages could demonstrate mastery of the particular behaviors measured on those imaginary CRTs. Then we'd have our cake and eat it too. We'd have "Norm Referenced Criterion Referenced Tests."

Why is this wonderful idea imaginary? Why hasn't a society that puts humans on the moon, that develops enough nuclear power to destroy the planet, that exchanges malfunctioning kidneys for healthy ones, developed such tests?

Is education really just another football game?

Why, indeed! Perhaps we don't like the idea that everyone would have access to being first. Perhaps closely monitored instruction would be so efficient that everyone would learn almost everything taught in school. Perhaps the elite would not be so elite anymore.

Or perhaps it's a way to maintain the competitive spirit that drives our aggressions. That spirit reduces education to a sort of ubiquitous football game whose purpose is to "beat your neighbor to the goal line." Perhaps football isn't really an ancillary of university education; perhaps the reverse is true — that college education is an ancillary of football and the name of the education game is competition, not learning.

With NRSTs driving the important decision making, we limit excellence to under 16% of the school population. If we dared to drive educational decision making with CRTs as integral parts of instruction, we might be so efficient that 99% of the school population would achieve excellence. Then who would be excluded from Harvard? Who would be dropped from medical school? Who would be allowed to become professors and develop tomorrow's definitions of excellence? Who would be left to be unemployed, to fill our jails, to do the boring, low-paying jobs?

What a lousy football game: there would be no losers!

Testing's Tower of Babel
(Or...confusion's the name of the game!)

The CIA and test makers

What do the CIA and the testing profession have in common? They both use secret codes. Other professions do it all the time. Physicians still write some prescriptions in Latin — or at least the handwriting is so illegible patients think it's Latin. Lawyers use a special form of obfuscated English for legal documents — woe to anyone who dares write a contract in plain English!

Not to be outdone, NRST experts have invented an elaborate Tower of Babel to maintain professional exclusivity and hide a host of sins. This chapter decodes the babble and exposes the shocking truth behind their decision to build that tower.

How to build a Tower of Babel

They didn't mean to build the tower. It just happened. Here's a six-part history of testing's Tower of Babel.

Part one: Discovering the obvious

Right after World War I, test makers decided to measure scholastic achievement with the old Stanford Binet Intelligence Test and the Otis Quick Scoring Test of Mental Abilities. They called those NRSTs "intelligence tests" (although now you know they weren't).

After administering those tests to many people, the test makers discovered what anyone without a Ph.D. in math could have told them: If we measure almost anything *that we do not manipulate or control*, and if the test population is large enough, a few will score high, an equal few will score low, and most will score somewhere around a particular value. We call that value "the average."

Are you surprised to learn that *unless we cause it to be otherwise*, when we measure a large number of almost anything, a few measures will be high, a few will be low, and the rest will be in the middle? How about height? Sex appeal? Nose length? Ability to say "Peter Piper picked a peck of pickled peppers" rapidly ten times?

We would *normally* expect such a result, *as long as we don't cause it to be otherwise*. So, in the case of test scores, we say the scores are *normally distributed*. But keep in mind that schools are places specificially designed to cause things to be otherwise.

Your great-grandmother (the one who didn't have a Ph.D. in math) would expect that if she cooked enough spaghetti for 100 contestants in a spaghetti-eating contest, a few would eat the most in the shortest time, a few would eat the least in the longest time, and most would eat an average amount at a rate somewhere between those extremes. As my great-grandmother would say: "That's normal."

Part two: Three little letters wreak havoc

To make sense out of the scores on those early intelligence tests, the experts analyzed the results as percentiles. That's percen*tiles* not percents. A percentile tells where a particular score falls in relation to other people's scores. These "other people" are called the *norm group*.

The reason NRSTs are called *norm referenced* is that, rather than telling what you know, their scores tell how you compare with others. They tell where your score falls in relation to *the norm*.

Suppose you got 37 correct out of 62 possible items on an NRST. That score would be compared with the norm group's scores and the report might come back as, for example: "You did as well as or better than 83% of the others taking the test."

But be careful! Don't confuse 83rd %ile with 83%.

You got 37 out of 62 items correct, about 60%. People in the norm who got 60% of the items correct on this test performed as well as or better than 83% of the *norm*. (I know this because I have all the norm group scores ranked in front of me.) They were at the 83rd %ile. Could three innocent letters, *i...l...e*, cause a Tower of Babel?

You bet they could! Teachers and students were confused. Percent and percentile even sounded the same. Lots of people couldn't cope with percent correct being a different value from percentile. For them, the words *percent* and *percentile* became babble.

Part three: Compounding the confusion

To relieve the confusion between the two, accommodating test makers decided to report NRST results in a different language, called *standard scores*.

They agreed to the following standard: *Call the 50th %ile 100; call the 84th %ile 115; call the 16th %ile 85.* And so on.

In other words (which is precisely what it was — other words), that score, known as the *average* — the score at which about half the norm group did as well as or better than the rest, and which percentiles would call the 50th %ile — was now called, by convention, 100. Those doing as well as or better than 16% of the norm were assigned the score of 85. Those doing as well as or better than 84% of the norm were assigned 115.

"That," reasoned the smart test makers, "should clear up the confusion between percent and percentile."

Unfortunately, it didn't. Now we had percents, percentiles and IQs. The tower builders now had three words for the same thing — three different terms for the same point on the ranking.

Part four: The confusion grows

At this point, confusion went from bad to worse. By

the end of World War II, schools had become so obsessed with testing that they wanted all kinds of tests beyond those wonders that had come to be called "intelligence tests."

Along came achievement tests, general scholastic aptitude tests, specific aptitude tests, attitude measures, vocational interest inventories, college board tests, etc. A testing avalanche almost buried teaching.

Each test maker wanted his or her own scoring language. College boards, for example, added a fourth language to the Tower of Babel. They called 100, 500. They called 115, 600. They called 85, 400. How's that for being unique?

Another test maker called the average 50. While college boards called the 84th %ile 600, and IQ test makers called it 115, this test maker called it 60. And so on. Chalk up another language. One IQ test maker decided to call his average 10 and his 84th %ile 13!

These new languages, or labeling systems, weren't entirely arbitrary. Once a system was arbitrarily assigned, it had an internal logic. So the test maker who designated the average 10 and the 84th %ile 13 called the 16th %ile 7. The difference between, for example, the 16th %ile and the 50th %ile was equal to the distance between the 50th %ile and the 84th %ile. Some test experts simplified their worlds by adapting the mathematical standard which calls the 50th %ile 0, the 16th %ile −1, and the 84th %ile +1.

Confusing? You ain't seen nothin' yet!

Part five: The grade level at last

By the 1950s, the confusion was so intense that commercial test makers feared a customer revolt. Percentile was the base; labeling variations for that base were the babble. But understanding that was apparently beyond the mathematical perspicacity of many school teachers. So the test makers invented a new number system, just for teachers, and for parents the teachers had trained to think like teachers: *the grade level.*

Actually, grade level scores were no different from the others. The test maker simply called the 50th %ile for the norm group of sixth graders, for example, a score of 6. Sixth graders' scores at the 84th %ile were called grade level score 8, because it appeared to be the average score for eighth graders. Before long, people were making such erroneous statements as: "According to the standardized test, this sixth-grade girl reads like an eighth-grader." Or, "According to the Martian Math Mentality Achievement Measure, Billy did three grade levels of work in six months of instruction."

What a mess! That sixth-grader did *not* read like an eighth-grader. Eighth-grade girls are beginning womanhood, and they do not read *The Scarlet Letter* the same way sixth-graders read it. Nor did Billy experience three years of life in six months. In both cases, all that happened was their scores on the tests ranked on or above the 84th %ile.

The new "grade level score" language was misleading and distorting, but it was simple. (We can easily live with our ignorance as long as we're not aware of it.) The other test score languages hung in there on their own turf. But for elementary and secondary schools, *grade level scores* rose above the cacophony to become the standard way to report school achievement and aptitude scores. Educators began to act as if a Bureau of Standards had some sort of *grade level* yardstick ensconced in the bowels of an official government building. This myth would have gone unchallenged and blissful ignorance would have prevailed had not ethics reared its troublesome head. The story continues in part six.

Part six: From confusion to chaos

All would have gone smoothly if some test makers' consciences hadn't begun to bother them. The issue was *reliability.* You recall that test reliability refers to how sure we are of the score's accuracy. In the 1960s, test makers discovered that, during their state of psychometric bliss, educators were making decisions about individual students based on these test scores. For example, students with scores of 115 IQ (scores at the 84th %ile) were being selected for special classes for the gifted, and students scoring at or below the 16th %ile were being shunted to special education classes.

More serious was the exclusion from gifted classes of kids with scores at the 83rd %ile, and the forced inclusion of others at the 15th %ile into classes for the retarded. Nor was this malpractice limited to grade schools. Top universities were eliminating applicants who scored, for example, 645 on the College Board Math Test when the school entrance requirement was 650.

Test makers knew that the most reliable NRSTs are not reliable enough to make these kinds of decisions. You will recall that test *validity* pertains to human decisions based on the test score. If a person's score is not reliable enough to make such decisions, but if educators use that unreliable score to make decisions, then the test's *validity* is at issue. NRSTs are never very reliable for an individual score. That led from confusion to chaos. Here's what happened.

An exercise in self-delusion

Let's pretend that the value 10 represents perfect test reliability, perfect accuracy. The American Psychological Association (APA) and the American Educational Research Association (AERA) expect commercially published NRSTs to be at least 8 or above.

Commercial publishers report reliabilities of about 9 to 9.5 on the 10 scale. Independent researchers find those tests to rate about 8 to 8.5. Neither 8 nor 9.5 on a 10 scale is as high a reliability as test makers would lead you to think. But that is the best they can get with NRSTs.

The reported reliabilities are generated by large groups, and the reliability values refer to the reliability of average scores, *not individual scores*. The reliability for an individual score is called the *Standard Error of Measurement*, SEM for short. If they were to report reliability as the SEM for each score, everyone would see how unreliable the best NRSTs are when estimating an individual score.

How reliable is reliable?

First, let's use one of the most widely used NRSTs in the United States. It reports a reliability of about 9. When we check that reliability, we get about 8.2. But let's give the publisher the benefit of the doubt and use a reliability value of 8.7. We will still discover how unreliable the standard for "good reliability" is. (Remember, this reliability value describes a group score, not an individual score.)

Second, this reliability value for the group is an index of the test score's stability *at the average*, not above or below average. The further a score is from the average, the less reliable it is.

Third, the SEM for an individual score that is above or below average is very low. That's an important point, since tests are most often used to make decisions about students who are above or below average. On this widely used test, a score as good as or better than 75% of the norm group (75th %ile) is so unreliable that the true score would be somewhere between the 69th and the 85th %ile!

That 75th %ile means that the *true* score lurks somewhere within a 16 %ile band. If you think that's bad, consider this question: How certain are we of the probability that the true score is somewhere in that 16 %ile band? If we could control fatigue and learning, and were to give the test to the student 100 times, 68 out of the 100 times the student would earn a score falling between the 69th %ile and the 85th %ile. In other words, the score could be outside that band 32 out of 100 times!

Let's look at another example. Pretend your eighth-grade daughter takes this very test. It has 40 items and she gets 25 correct. According to the test manual, the test reliability is "high" (around 9). According to the same manual, a score of 25 out of 40 items for eighth-graders means that she performed as well as or better than 84% of the norm group. She is at the 84th %ile. But the standard error of an individual score at the 84th %ile on this "highly reliable" test means that her *true* score is somewhere within a 14 %ile band. That's a lot of slippage! (Remember, that's an example of a test with the highest reliability one could expect to get on a typical aptitude or achievement NRST.)

Good reliability is at best low reliability for individual scores. So commercial test makers put their best foot forward: they advertise their group reliability values for large groups and keep the SEMs of individual scores quiet. They can't completely hide those SEMs because the arithmetic formula for SEM is in the public domain. However, neither teachers nor parents run around with calculators poised to estimate SEM from the published reliability data. So educators get away with making decisions based on these test scores, and the ones who suffer are our kids.

Meanwhile, teachers are also making decisions about individual children using these "highly reliable" NRSTs. Consider what self-delusion this is! With the best reliability, an NRST score is grossly inaccurate. What are the test makers doing about it?

Wrestling with problems of conscience

Test makers are human. They know their definitions of test reliability are fatuous. Having converted percentiles to grade levels so that teachers could understand NRST scores, they began to suffer pangs of conscience. They realized that making test scores easy to understand caused teachers to use the highly unreliable individual scores to make life-shaping decisions about kids.

Conscience-stricken test experts knew they had

deluded themselves into thinking that 9 was very reliable because it was the best they could do. But they also knew that if the general public understood the issue (that the best they could get was bad), their entire profession would be in danger. They found themselves torn between large profits and ethical behavior. Cleverly, they tried to steer a course between capitalism and conscience. They added another language to their Tower of Babel. Rather than eliminate the test, they devised a plan whereby scores would become so confusing to teachers that they would no longer be able to make decisions.

Oh NO! Not more!

Oh yes, lots more. They decided to replace grade levels with a new system called *stanines*. A student's score was not a point on the percentile range. Instead it was *somewhere in one of nine bands* — but no one could say exactly where.

The intent of this ploy was to make users think of an NRST score as a band rather than a specific point. Obviously, it didn't work. Even at the height of the stanine fad, many school guidance counselors were translating stanines back into percentiles and grade level scores so teachers and parents would understand them.

Along with stanines came more gimmicks to confuse test users, under the assumption that it was better to confuse than to misuse, but that misuse was better for profits than no use. Test scores were reported as z scores, Z scores, AGCT scores, and an endless variety of other systems called "normalized standard scores." If this sounds like Laurel and Hardy comedy, you're partly right. However, the resemblance ends with consideration of the seriousness of this attempt to save the tests at any cost, even when the cost was our children.

The current status of the tower

Confusion reigns. Misuse continues to run rampant. As we wind down the 20th century, the tower has ceased to grow, but it's holding its own. Most schools are back to percentiles and grade level scores, refusing to admit to themselves how inaccurate these individual scores are. The other babble continues, each language maintaining its unique turf.

Meanwhile, as NRST sales soar, the SEM issue is locked in the closet. More schools than ever before use NRSTs to make decisions about individuals, and they are no more reliable than they have been over the past decade. In fact, NRSTs reached their upper limits of reliability about a decade ago.

Faced with this reality, we have a choice: use these tests for large group data only, eliminate them before they hurt another generation of kids, or ignore the truth and continue to misuse them.

Review

The purpose of this chapter is to increase the probability that every reader knows 12 things about NRSTs, so that, if a test of those 12 things were given, there would *not* be a normal distribution of test scores. To make sure our CRT doesn't cause a ranking among you, please read these 12 points before you take the following Can Do Test. (I'll do anything to be a successful teacher. I'll even give you the answers! But then, that's what you pay for, isn't it?)

- A normal distribution of test scores means that a few get high scores, an equal few get low scores, and most get scores in the middle.

- Those middle scores are called "the average."

- When we measure almost anything, we'll get a normal distribution of scores, if we haven't arranged events to prevent such a distribution. In education, that means we can design instruction to be so ineffective that it doesn't make enough difference to prevent a normal distribution. Or we can teach so we guarantee some will learn and some will fail, and we'll get a normal distribution. Or we can teach everyone everything they need to know to get all the test items correct. Only the latter will prevent a normal distribution. It's called effective teaching.

● The "bright idea" of this book is simple (I'll say more about this in the last chapter): *The purpose of formal instruction should be to change learners so that scores on measures of learning outcomes are not normally distributed!*

● The earliest NRSTs were used to rank students from high to low, or vice versa, depending on which direction you like to travel. The easiest way to report a point in the ranking was with percentiles. For example, Billy sank 6 out of 10 basketball throws from the foul line. That's 60% accuracy. To know how good that is, we compare him with the rest of his teammates, the "norm." When we rank all the players' scores, we find that Billy did as well as or better than 80% of his "reference" group. He was at the 80th %ile.

● Since educators, parents and students confused percent accuracy and the percentile score, test experts invented a different language for the same score. They called the new language IQ. But it was merely a different labeling system for the rankings.

● By the 1950s, schools were flooded with all kinds of NRSTs besides "intelligence" tests. They had achievement tests, aptitude tests, college entrance exams, and so on. If educators had bothered to look closely at the test items, they would have discovered that the same kinds of items were showing up on tests with different names. At any rate, IQ language became confusing. So test publishers invented another new language called *grade level score*.

● The crunch came when NRST makers began to fear for their souls. (That happens when old age begins to set in.) They knew how unreliable an individual's NRST score was. To report a kid's score as 3.7 grade level was a lie. It would more accurately be a score somewhere between, for example, grade level score 2 and grade level score 4.5. Saving the profits from NRST sales was more important than saving their souls, so they didn't want to advertise each score's standard error of measurement. Instead, they tried to hide the score slippage in a new language called *stanines*, which were bands rather than inaccurate points on a scale.

- By the 1970s, the Tower of Babel soared to its present height. We had percentiles, grade level scores, IQ scores, z scores, Z scores, AGCT scores, normalized standard scores, stanines and a host of other codes. They all represented different labels for the same ranking on a scale of low to high, leaving educators in total confusion. Test users finally retreated to the safe grade level scores and percentiles. NRST sales soared, and the profits soothed the pangs of conscience. The use of stanines waned.

- We were left with what we always had: Reliability values bandied about by the test experts represented score stability for large group averages. Individual NRST scores remained grossly unreliable.

- NRSTs are about as reliable as they'll ever be. That's bad news, because the best isn't good enough to warrant the use of individual scores to make important decisions about people.

- The further away from the test norm average an individual score is, the greater its standard error of measurement.

- Since test scores are most often used to make decisions about individuals significantly below or above average, and since that's where the individual scores are least reliable, one wonders why more angry parents haven't found more lawyers clever enough to prove damages against school personnel who've ruined a kid's life by misusing these scores.

A Can Do Test

Choose one correct answer for each of the following items, unless told otherwise (which is often the case).

1. After teaching about testing's Tower of Babel, we give a CRT. About 16% of test scores turn out to be above average. Another 16% are below average, and about two-thirds are around the average. We say the:
    a. test was too easy.
    b. test was too hard.
    c. scores were normally distributed.

2. We say the:
    a. teaching was effective.
    b. teaching was not too effective.

3. In education we can expect a normal distribution of test scores when the teacher (choose 2 — look out now!):
    a. manipulates learners, so everyone performs the same on the test.
    b. manipulates learners, so everyone does not perform the same on the test.
    c. doesn't teach effectively, so everyone does not perform the same on the test.

4. In question 3, which would we blame for the normal distribution?
    a. The teacher.
    b. Chance.

5. NRST scores (choose 3 — no, I'm not kidding):
    a. discriminate.
    b. rank.
    c. compare scores to norms.

6. Which is a percentile?
    a. A ranking.
    b. 6 out of 10 = 60%.

7. Which statement could be correct?
    a. 40% correct equals the 98th %ile.
    b. If you get 7 out of 10 correct on any test, your score must be in the 70th %ile.

8. Here are four NRST results:
    100 IQ
    average score
    50th %ile
    grade level score of 9 for a 9th grader on day 1
    These results are all:
    a. different labels for the same rank.
    b. different scores on the same test.

9. The NRST makers' Tower of Babel refers to the many different:
    a. tests in use.
    b. labels for the same rank.

10. What piqued test experts' consciences?
    a. High test reliability values for large groups.
    b. Group average scores.
    c. Large SEMs for individual scores.

11. The further above average an individual's NRST score, the:
    a. lower the measurement error.
    b. higher the measurement error.

12. The further below average an individual's NRST score, the:
    a. lower the measurement error.
    b. higher the measurement error.

13. The cut-off test score for entrance to Polly Prissy's Private School for Prosperous Precocious Pupils is the 90th %ile on an IQ test. Poor Patty Pooper scores at the 89th %ile. "Too dumb for this school," rules Polly Prissy. Mrs. Pooper says, "I read Dr. Cohen's book and:
    a. Patty's true IQ could be as high as the 99th %ile."
    b. I don't believe percentiles really exist."

14. One conclusion we can reasonably draw from this chapter about using NRST scores to make an educational decision about an individual high or low achiever is:
    a. do.
    b. don't.

15. The "bright idea" in this chapter is that instruction (choose 3):
    a. can make achievement scores distribute normally.
    b. can make achievement scores not distribute normally.
    c. should make achievement scores not distribute normally.

You probably don't need feedback for items 2, 3 and 4, but it's an opportunity to repeat, for the tenth time, that *effective instruction eliminates a normal distribution of test scores*. Everyone should be competent — if not, scores will distribute normally. In that case, blame the teacher for letting chance overcome effective instruction. Another way of saying it (for the eleventh time) is that if instruction causes scores to distribute normally, we should blame the teacher!

Problems of validity

When profits are the purpose, only fools allow facts to stand in the way. Test makers are no fools, so the use of unreliable NRST scores continues to be endemic. In chapter four we saw that test users often make decisions based on unreliable scores from tests that don't measure what the user thinks they measure. Now we'll consider other test validity problems found in the various types of NRSTs schools use.

Achievement tests

Achievement tests come in all shapes and sizes: reading, math, English, foreign languages, social studies, science, vocabulary, etc. As we saw before, test validity refers to *what people do* with test results, not to the test itself. Achievement test users tend to believe three fallacies.

Evaluating teaching and curriculum

It's a fallacy to think achievement tests can evaluate teaching or curriculum. The problem is that most NRSTs are too insensitive to reliably measure teaching or assess how well a curriculum works. Remember, NRSTs are forced to sample from *a large body of behaviors*, because individual educators are imprecise about what they teach. If we can't specify exactly what is taught, then the test of what is taught is bound to be insensitive. Problems arise when people uncritically decide to draw conclusions about much smaller groups.

Sometimes achievement NRSTs do detect teaching effects, and sometimes they just *look* as if they detect teaching effects. In the first case, we're usually dealing with a rare situation in which students make enormous gains. In the second case, we're usually dealing with a statistical artifact known as "regression to the average."

Regression to the average occurs when the students tested are very low achievers to begin with. Given the test's error measurement, its slippage has to move in the up direction, since there's little room to move down. So the error measurement causes the average score to move up, making it appear that the students gained in achievement.

Of course, the reverse happens if students are very high achievers to begin with. After instruction, the achievement NRST makes them appear to have decreased in achievement, because the error measurement has more room to move the scores down than up.

School administrators in high-achieving districts do themselves and their teachers a great disservice if they use NRSTs to assess their efforts. Regression to the average is bound to make them look bad every few years. Inversely, school administrators in low-achieving districts need only hold the quality of their programs constant. Over a period of time, regression to the average is bound to occur a few times to make them look more effective than they really are.

Occasionally, NRST achievement gains occur as sampling accidents. Some of the precise behaviors taught by a teacher accidentally show up in a few test items. But the body of behaviors an NRST samples encompasses an enormous corpus of possibilities. To attempt assessment samples against such odds is poor poker.

The problem is that many educators use NRSTs to measure instructional effects year to year. How absurd! The accidental overlap between behaviors learned in the classroom and the same behaviors appearing in the NRST items takes years and large numbers of classrooms to show up. Any teacher or principal would be a fool to allow such a test to evaluate his or her effectiveness. But there are fools out there.

Obviously, CRTs in which items represent the precise behaviors taught in the classroom would be more useful assessment tools. It doesn't take a pedagogical genius to figure out that measuring precisely what was taught is a more accurate way to monitor instruction than measuring samples which may or may not include what was taught. One wonders why this hasn't occurred to thousands of school administrators who continue to use NRSTs to monitor their schools. One wonders even more why teachers allow their bosses to evaluate them on tests that are usually mismatched with what they teach.

Teaching the mundane

It's a fallacy to think that teaching the behaviors tested on commercially published achievement NRSTs will provide a solution, although it has been done with enormous success and dramatic efficiency in some research conducted recently.

Unfortunately, the result is not very educational, since NRSTs tend to measure the mundane. NRSTs are designed to be administered to thousands of test takers. They are scored by machines. The items are limited to true/false, multiple choice, and similar "easy to print and score" formats. Many teachers, on the other hand, try to teach more important behaviors. In other words, commercially published NRSTs tend to measure the mundane while teachers try to teach the substantive.

A good reading teacher trains students to laugh in response to a funny story. A few tears are an appropriate response to a sad story. But neither laughs nor tears are readable by an optical scanner used to score NRSTs.

A social studies achievement NRST can easily measure if an American student knows that July 4 is Independence Day. But no social studies NRST measures how well a student appreciates an opposing point of view in a discussion of government foreign policy.

A CRT, on the other hand, can measure whatever the teacher chooses as an important learning outcome. In the "appreciating a point of view" example, teachers can list "behavioral indicators" (things they want to see students do) that indicate appreciation of an opposing viewpoint in a discussion about current affairs. Then they can

observe the presence, absence and/or frequency of those
behavioral indicators.

If we continue to use NRSTs to monitor instruction,
might the school curriculum eventually match the
NRSTs? What a dreadful thought! That would be a
triumph of the mundane.

But it happens because admin is score driven

Disregarding the excess baggage

The most insidious fallacy of all is to think we can
ignore the "excess baggage" contained in achievement
tests. If we spot an educator or psychologist using an
individual's unreliable NRST score to force an important
decision, we can blow the whistle. When educational
administrators use NRST scores to evaluate teaching, we
can go to court or call out union pickets. But unless
you're a trained behavior analyst, you'll miss the "excess
baggage" of test items that have nothing to do with what
the test purports to measure, items that account —
according to the research — for 20% to 40% of NRST
score differences.

All pencil/paper NRST and CRT items test "general
school smartness" in addition to whatever else the item is
supposed to measure. Remember, the original Stanford
Binet Intelligence Test was designed to separate out
students who had learned how to succeed in the
elementary grades well enough for the state to invest in
their secondary school education. They were "school
smart."

Recent research is just beginning to tease out of test
items the behaviors underlying "school smarts." We call
one group of such behaviors "test wiseness." Test wiseness
training causes test takers to budget their time while
taking a test. Test-wise students make intelligent guesses
when they don't know an answer. They learn to eliminate
obviously wrong answers, thereby increasing the
probability of guessing correctly. And shrewd test takers
don't always do what test directions tell them to do. As a
result, they often do better than those less shrewd. Notice,

test-wise students don't know more answers; nor do they have "higher achievement" in what the test purports to measure. But they do have superior "beat the system" skills.

For example, a reading test typically directs the test taker to "first read the passage and then answer the questions that follow." Smart test takers reverse the directions; first they read the questions and then they read the passage. They read to find the answers.

Kids who have learned a dozen or so of these beat-the-system behaviors seem to get higher scores. So it's evident the tests are measuring things other than what they're intended to. In our research, when test takers are taught some of these beat-the-system skills, without increasing their achievement in reading, or math, or social studies, or whatever the test score is supposed to be measuring, they achieve significantly large increases in their scores. For example, in one recent study we spent only two 30-minute lessons training second-graders to read the questions before reading the passage. After the training, they took the NRST and their scores jumped from the 50th %ile to the 90th %ile.

Roberto provides a good example of another category of excess baggage we call "extra cognitive load." This term signifies that other thinking skills beyond what we're trying to measure influence the score.

The second-grade "reading" NRST asked Roberto to select (out of three) the best word for an accompanying illustration. That's one of the mundane behaviors commercially published NRSTs call "reading."

The illustration was a simple line drawing of a dog running down a winding path. The three options from which Roberto had to select were (in order from left to right): *sun...fun...run.* Roberto selected *fun.* The "best" correct answer, said the test publisher, was *run.* Roberto got the item wrong, which on a reading test means the child can't read the item.

Immediately after the test, I interviewed Roberto as part of a research study on excess baggage. I pointed to the word *sun* and asked: "Why didn't you choose this?" (Notice, I neither said the word nor asked Roberto to say it.)

Roberto responded: "'Cause there ain't no sun in the picture." This was in fact the case. Obviously, he could read (which means understand) the word *sun*.

When I pointed to the word *fun* and asked why he chose it, Roberto pointed to the dog's tail, around which the illustrator had drawn action lines depicting movement. As I looked at the action lines, it was obvious that they were equally interpretable as tail-wagging indicators or body-movement indicators. Apparently, Roberto chose to perceive them as tail wagging, a commonly accepted symbol of a happy dog. No question about it. Roberto knew the dog was having fun! And I had to agree.

Even more interesting was his response to my question, "Why didn't you choose this word?" pointing to the last word, *run*. After all, that was the word the test maker said was the correct answer. Again, I neither said the word nor asked him to say it. His response was, "I could have."

Roberto was quite a reader! But according to the test score, he was unable to read the item. His score on that item was generated by excess baggage, not by reading. But the school interpreted it as an indication of Roberto's reading ability. In this case, the excess baggage helped ensure that the test would discriminate among Roberto and his classmates even if they were well taught. That's a *validity* issue.

Research indicates that all tests are loaded with excess baggage. What makes it *excess* is that it's irrelevant to reading and, therefore, not likely to be taught. In that study in which Roberto was a subject, we found about a dozen strange behaviors children needed to be able to perform in order to do well on reading achievement NRSTs commonly used in schools — none of them reading behaviors. All together, excess baggage accounted for as much as 30% of differences among test takers' scores.

What happens when educators make decisions about the children or the reading programs in their schools based on such test results? Obviously, those decisions involve a significant amount of invalidity.

Aptitude tests

Validity problems for aptitude tests are identical to those for achievement tests. That's because the fundamental difference between the two is the interpretation of scores. The test items are identical. The same type of item Roberto got on his reading achievement NRST shows up on the second-grade reading aptitude test. The difference is that the user interprets the achievement score as a measure of what the learner *has* learned, the aptitude score as a measure of what the learner *could* learn in the future. Since the items are the same, the achievement test fallacies apply equally to the aptitude test.

Test makers sell two types of aptitude tests, general and specific. Schools purchase general scholastic aptitude tests to make decisions about which kids will (their words) "benefit most from being placed in special classes," as one example. Once again, the SEM problem is hidden in the closet. Specific aptitude tests assess achievement in specific areas such as math, spatial relations, clerical facility, foreign language, etc.

Aptitude tests are not as popular as they used to be, and certainly not as widely used as achievement NRSTs. After all, they are no different from the achievement tests. In order to predict how well people will do in the future, we test their achievement now. Then we assume that if they are outstanding mathematicians now, they will probably be so in the future. Apparently school administrators caught on to the scam over the years and figured out that the achievement NRSTs would do the same thing as the aptitude NRSTs.

I wonder why it took them so long? I wonder why some administrators still haven't figured it out?

Aptitude test score interpretations carry another characteristic that makes them even more dangerous than achievement test score interpretations. Educators and parents think these tests measure what students *can* or *can't* learn, or the *level* to which they can develop a specific aptitude. For over a quarter of a century, the research indicates that aptitude tests are simply predictors of "learning rate." A low math aptitude score doesn't indicate that Johnny can't learn calculus. If that score were accurate (which it isn't), it would simply predict that Johnny might take longer to learn calculus than others who have a higher aptitude score.

IQ tests

IQ tests are general scholastic aptitude tests. One additional fact is pretty clear: Since they are aptitude tests, and since aptitude tests are achievement tests, and since achievement tests measure what we have learned — albeit not always in school — then the knowledge and skills we call IQ are not innate. When an IQ test asks: "How far is it from St. Louis to Chicago?" there's no evidence of the answer existing in the DNA code. If a child knows the word *flavor*, no evidence exists linking that knowledge to genes. The ability to string beads, manipulate interlocking puzzles, answer arithmetic problems correctly, be able to say as many words as possible in 30 seconds — none of these behaviors appears to be genetically inherited from one's parents.

College entrance tests

College entrance tests are aptitude tests. And aptitude tests are achievement tests. What more can we say about them that hasn't already been said?

Criterion Referenced Tests

CRTs can be invalid too. They can test the mundane. They can carry excess baggage. They are, after all, achievement tests. But they aren't NRSTs. Their major function is not to rank, but to test precisely what is taught. A CRT is valid if its items match the behaviors that are taught.

Good CRTs are hard to find because they depend upon clear definitions of what is taught. Since educators are notoriously imprecise about what they teach, we tend to see lots of mundane, irrelevant and invalid CRTs. In fact, most CRTs we see in schools are NRSTs in CRT disguise.

What do we want our kids to be?

Are you beginning to detect a bias? Do you get the feeling, in spite of the last paragraph in the previous chapter, that this book is a disguised sales pitch for CRTs?

Not true! The real issue is the purpose of schooling. NRSTs and CRTs represent sharply different viewpoints about the purpose of schools. Whatever people may *say* they believe schooling to be, watch what they do. Watch what they do with test results in particular, and you'll discover what they really perceive as the purpose of schooling.

The NRST's view of schooling

An NRST's survival on the test market depends on its ability to differentiate among test takers. The testing profession uses a statistical technique called "correlation" to arithmetically demonstrate an NRST's validity. It "correlates" NRST scores with scores on some criterion of validity.

There's an amusing hitch to this. The criterion of validity of a new NRST of, say, reading achievement, is usually the old NRST it's replacing, or one from a competing publisher. In other words, the test maker proves his new NRST really measures reading because it correlates with his old NRST, or with a competitor's NRST. Catch 22.

The statistical correlation formula *demands* a normal distribution of test scores. To put it bluntly, if the NRST doesn't divide test takers into a few excellent ones, a few hopeless ones, and a large mass of mediocre ones spread between the extremes, it *cannot* be valid. That is an arithmetic fact.

IQ tests, college board aptitude tests, the ubiquitous norm referenced standardized achievement tests, and all the other NRSTs validated in this manner have become woven into the basic fabric of our educational practices. Presuming that model=fact, we teach to ensure that failure and mediocrity characterize 85% of our students. We use two methods to guide that teaching:

- Teach poorly enough so we cause the normal distribution.
- Test so enough non-taught factors (excess baggage) sneak in to ensure chance distribution of scores. Chance gives us "normal" distribution.

By policy, we not only expect but require our teaching efforts to generate a normal distribution of results. As we've seen, this assumption has subverted every aspect of schooling to the extent that normal teaching practices embrace ineffective instruction.

A telling contrast

Consider the following contrasts between education derived from the NRST perspective and that based on a CRT viewpoint.

NRSTs: Don't show students test questions before the test. Don't "give away the answers." Make tests "secure." We call this the Pentagon Phenomenon.

CRTs: Show students the questions so they know what they need to know before being taught and tested. This guarantees that nearly everyone will get a perfect score.

NRSTs: To teach what we test and test what we teach is cheating.

CRTs: Good instruction tests what's taught and teaches what's tested. Therefore, we should think critically about what's worth teaching.

NRSTs: Some students just can't learn everything we teach.

CRTs: Every student can learn everything we teach, given appropriate instruction and sufficient time to learn.

Choosing a course of action

Think of test validity as a way of recasting this question: What is the purpose of schooling?

If your answer is "to create an elite, to ensure that a few will excel, a few will fail, and the mass will remain mediocre," then NRSTs are the best tools to fulfill your purpose.

If your answer is "to make everyone excel," then roll up your sleeves and begin immediately to replace those fuzzies that educators like to hide behind when someone asks what their goals are. In other words, decide what excellence looks like and develop CRTs to test it. Then teach to those tests.

What do we want our kids to be?

What's worth teaching is ultimately a value judgment, and values are always a matter of opinion. However, one thing is not a matter of opinion. The law requires us to submit all children to education either in state-controlled public schools or in private schools. And since we parents have a right to know what the state intends to make of our children, schools must state their outcomes clearly and publicly.

Each of us should be able to see clearly what our schools have decided to make our children be. From the educator's point of view, to clearly display outcomes is an ethical responsibility. From the community's perspective, to clearly display outcomes is an act of accountability. From a technical perspective, the clearest display of a school's values is not what it says its outcomes are, but the assessments it uses to decide the educational fate of our children.

Whatever rationalizations we use to deny the power of tests in our society, the fact is that those tests reflect what we want our children to be. Do we want excellence, or do we want the mundane? Do we want to continue limiting excellence to the privileged few? Do we want to continue disguising some outcomes as excess baggage? Do we want to continue using inaccurate assessments to make critical decisions about our children?

These are accountability issues, and accountability is the core of ethical responsibility. Unless educators, parents and school governing boards recognize that these are also testing issues, we will continue to produce a normal distribution of mundane instructional results. And we will continue to destroy thousands of children by using inaccurate assessments to make critical educational decisions.

On the other hand, if we clearly define what we want our schools to produce and design our assessments to match those definitions, both teaching and measuring those outcomes will be a lot easier than most people realize. The tough job is deciding what excellence is. What *do* we want our kids to be?

So why hasn't the CRT bandwagon swept the planet?

Some of the people who are disheartened by the misuse of NRSTs are equally discouraged by the misuse of CRTs. Ironically, many of them basically agree with the principles that underlie CRTs:

- We must be professionally accountable.
- We must monitor our effects on our students.
- We must think of schooling as educating students, not discriminating among them.
- We must think deeply and continuously about what is worth teaching.
- We must teach under the assumption that almost everyone in school can learn almost anything that we can clearly define as our instructional outcome.

Yet these critics shudder with dismay at the thought of CRTs. There are two major reasons for their concerns — one perfectly valid, the other grounded in misunderstanding. The first has to do with the fact that CRTs have been drowning students in oceans of paper/pencil tests of the mundane. The second is based on a disagreement concerning the definability of substantive instructional outcomes. CRT critics know that the more important outcomes of learning are not easily definable, but CRT advocates aren't quick to admit that. I have a notion, however, there may be less disagreement than first meets the eye.

Measuring the mundane

Most CRTs currently used in schools measure the same kind of behaviors as NRSTs — paper/pencil skills. Teachers who know CRTs only through their experience with the corruptions of the concept now in vogue in many school districts are right in criticizing them as measures of the mundane.

For example, a recent study of American schools

found that CRTs monitoring reading instruction across the continent at best assess only mundane, and often irrelevant, skills. Almost no schools accept *teacher observations* of substantive reading behaviors as "legitimate measures" of reading achievement. Apparently school systems don't allow observational data to carry the same importance as a numerical score from a paper/pencil test, and this attitude increases the probability of measuring the mundane.

In a paper/pencil environment, CRTs are subject to the same constrictions as NRSTs, workbooks and textbooks: educational outcomes are less substantive. This is not a result of the CRT movement, however, but of a long-standing paper/pencil grip on schools. CRTs have been victims of it, not a cause.

Victim or cause, CRTs deserve the disdain of their critics for perpetuating the trashing of minds and spirits caused by what we too often teach and test in classrooms. Surely schooling *should* lead to something more akin to the human potential, something more than being able to select the best statement of a main idea, spell *i-e* words correctly, or name the capital cities of Europe.

But the critics may be focusing their wrath on the wrong source of the problem. Attacking CRTs relieves the true culprits — those teachers, administrators and publishers who design instructional programs that teach the mundane — from the pressure to reform.

How ironic that two perspectives can agree on the same evil but see it in directly opposite ways. For one, CRTs are the cause; for the other, they are the solution. What both sides oppose is the mundane learning that so many children are asked to accept day after day. That evil existed long before the CRT movement came along and was, in fact, exposed by it. CRTs have dramatically advertised the list of mundane skills monopolizing western schools. But instead of destroying the evil, I see some of my colleagues intent on destroying the messenger.

Defining the undefinables

Obviously many of the more substantive educational outcomes don't lend themselves to pencil/paper tests. They must be observed in student behaviors. Such observations measure the criterion outcomes of instruction that matter most to us. Vicariously sharing Raskalnikov's despair, discovering symmetry in calculus equations, recognizing familiar themes in Ted Geisel's children's books, loving learning — these are examples of the educational outcomes we most desire. They must be taught, tracked and assessed. But most challenging of all, they must be defined. And therein lies the fundamental source of misunderstanding between CRT advocates and critics. How do we define what appears to be undefinable?

Perhaps we can make those undefinables definable if we make two commitments, one technical and the other philosophic.

The *technical* commitment trains teachers first to observe behaviors and then to use their observations to define in operational terms those human qualities most often considered "spiritual entities." For example:

- What do lovers of art and biology look like that causes us to recognize them? How do they behave?
- When we say that students manifest an "appreciation of or tolerance for ambiguity in the human character," what do we see those students *do* that generates that description?

Providing operational descriptions does not de-spiritualize the spiritual. It merely specifies some *behavioral indicators* of those undefinable qualities, which in turn become the CRT "test items," so to speak. They are what we want to see our students do as a result of our instructional efforts.

The *philosophic* commitment underlying the technical one involves two aspects. First, CRT advocates reject the "truth by faith" perspective which argues that, since certain instructional outcomes are undefinable, it must be accepted on faith that:

● what we teach is worth learning;
● what we teach is what we *say* we teach (that is, there's perfect matching of what we say we do, what we do, and the effect on our students of what we do);
● students we so designate have learned "it" even if we can't define "it." Others we designate have not learned it.

Instead, the CRT perspective requires clear criteria of mastery — clear behavioral indicators of assessment, written or observed. Valuable or not, the outcomes taught, sought and measured are made operational, and we can debate their value.

Second and most important, *operational definitions of a learned human quality are NOT the same thing as that quality*. They are merely behavioral indicators that *more or less* indicate the presence or absence of that quality. For example, loving to read mystery novels is a human quality that one may choose to teach, or choose to observe in a student. Such a quality is usually assigned to a person who:

● selects mystery stories over other types of reading;
● prefers reading mystery stories to doing math or science homework;
● gives evidence of having read scores of such novels;
● hides an Agatha Christie novel in her geography book...and so on.

In other words, as behavioral indicators, all outcomes are definable. However, such definitions are not definitive. We must be willing to accept them as value judgments about the qualities we seek, not as immutable, universal, Platonic entities. In fact, when we make our fuzzies operational, we must feel the limitations of our humanity. Our behavioral indicators almost always fall short of what we *feel* lies within a human quality. So we find ourselves constantly striving for better, clearer, more satisfying indicators.

Thus, the philosophic commitment is to a never-ending search for better indicators. Whether we accept this striving or reject it because it *is* never-ending determines the difference between professional accountability and the lack of it. Such a commitment redefines teaching as a philosophic quest.

The teacher as philosopher

It may sound corny, but education is a philosophic enterprise. Classroom management aside, the *teaching* component of education is a relatively easy task. When the outcome is defined operationally, the methodology is relatively easy to design and deliver. In 35 years of designing and delivering instructional systems to classrooms throughout the world, I've found few teachers who can't develop effective methods.

But I have also observed that most teachers are confused about the relationship between their effective methods and what they thought their students had learned. In other words, the difficulty is not *how* to teach, but *what* to teach. The error we often make is to forget that what we teach is anything more specific than an ongoing process of philosophic inquiry into the nature of those things we value most. When what we teach is easy to define, we are probably teaching the mundane and avoiding confrontation with outcomes that matter.

The CRT approach recognizes education as a never-ending search for instructional outcomes worth pursuing. The fact that the process of defining substantive outcomes must remain open-ended does not mean that we don't, at specific points in our instructional efforts, have a clear picture of the desired outcomes. We know what the indicators are, however dissatisfied we may be with them.

What are the alternatives?

We can either try to know what we're doing when we teach, or not. In either case, we affect the lives of others.

It's often true, when we interact with others, that we are not doing with them (or to them) what we think we are. That's the nature of ordinary human interaction. But teaching is meant to be more than ordinary human interaction. Teaching requires *professional* behavior that goes beyond the ordinary, that includes the responsibility of knowing what we're doing to others. In a sense, it's a decision to burden ourselves with something like ongoing self-psychoanalysis.

Faced with this burden, what choices do we have? We can proclaim our ordinary behavior to be extraordinary by claiming *spiritual* validity, asking ourselves as well as our students to take on faith our inherent ability to "do what's worth doing" — rather like a clergyman without a bible. Or we can assume the responsibility of defining what we do, which requires ongoing monitoring of both our own and our students' behaviors, as well as a continuous redefinition of our indicators — a CRT process.

Education should be a learning, not a discriminating process. Schools will be more effective, and our society more humane, if we approach testing from a CRT perspective. But if we do, we must learn to be comfortable with the unending nature of the task and the elusive nature of instructional outcomes worth seeking — comfortable with ambiguity, but not complacent, because we'll continue to be dissatisfied with our current indicators, even as we strive to redefine them. *Our* behavior must indicate our belief that a test score should *not* be a mark for life.

As the Education function has been
given to "Experts" the teacher
becomes a monitor rather than educator -
Book tests - WS - Skill pacs - Enrichment
+ Remediation - Scripted lessons etc.

Only when you throw away the packaged
Stuff can you get CRT -

But what about the administra that
fill your day?

creativity needs to come
back to teaching -
creativity in presentation
                    evaluation

we tend to differ to experts
—

The *Bright Idea* Series

In *Bright Idea* books, gifted authors reveal to readers the hearts of their professional lives. What has excited them professionally? What have they spent their years discovering, and why?

In these books they dress some old truths in new styles, and reveal some new truths about children, about language, about learning, about teachers, teaching and parenting.

The series was conceived and is published in Canada, but the authors come from all over: the United States, New Zealand, The Netherlands, Great Britain, Canada.

So far twelve titles have been published:

☞	**The Craft of Children's Writing**	Judith Newman
	Grand Conversations: **Literature Groups in Action**	Ralph Peterson and Maryann Eeds
	Learning Computer Learning	Veronica Buckley and Martin Lamb
	Other Countries, Other Schools	Mike Bruce
☞	**Reading Begins at Birth**	David B. Doake
☞	**Spel . . . Is a Four-Letter Word**	J. Richard Gentry
	Tests: Marked for Life?	S. Alan Cohen
	The Tone of Teaching	Max van Manen
☞	**What's Whole in Whole Language?**	Ken Goodman
	When School Is a Struggle	Curt Dudley-Marling
☞	**Whole Language: Inquiring Voices**	Dorothy Watson, Carolyn Burke and Jerome Harste
	A Word is a Word . . . Or Is It?	Michael Graves

In Canada, order from Scholastic Canada Ltd., 123 Newkirk Road, Richmond Hill, Ontario L4C 3G5.

In the United States, order from Scholastic Inc., P.O. Box 7502, Jefferson City, MO 65102.

☞ Available in New Zealand and Australia through Ashton Scholastic, and in the United Kingdom through Scholastic Publications.